The Ultimate Golf Quiz

Lagoon Books

Series Editor: Heather Dickson

Research: Sheila Harding

Additional contributors: Matthew Hirtes,
Peter Kirkham, Ann Marangos

Photographs: Sportsphoto Ltd

Page design and layout: Linley Clode

Cover design: Gary Inwood Studios

Published by:
LAGOON BOOKS
PO BOX 311, KT2 5QW, UK

ISBN: 1899712739

© LAGOON BOOKS, 1999

Lagoon Books is a trade mark of
Lagoon Trading Company Limited.
All rights reserved.

Printed in Singapore

The Ultimate
Golf Quiz

LAGOON
BOOKS

Introduction

With questions on everything from golfing terminology to famous golfing quotes, this book is an all-round-winner with something for everyone in it.

If you didn't know that you'd find Rae's Creek in Augusta, then perhaps you'd know where to find The Babe in the Woods or The Cardinal Bunker?

Similarly, if you didn't know that a guttie was a type of ball and fescue a type of grass, then perhaps you know the meaning of an albatross or an eagle? Better still, do you know how many pimples there are on a golf ball? Who's known as "The Walrus"? Or which club's known as a spoon?

For similar questions and much, much more, read on....

...but if you're clued up and feeling competitive, why not tee-off for the ultimate golf challenge and keep score as you read through the book?

SCORING: If the question has only one answer, score 8 points. If the question has eight separate answers, score 1 point for each answer you get correct. At the end of the book, add up your score and see how you fared.

> **Between 224 and 280 = Bogie**
> **Between 280 and 336 = Par**
> **Between 336 and 392 = Birdie**
> **Between 392 and 448 = Eagle**
> **Between 448 and 559 = Albatross**
> **A perfect score of 560 = A hole-in-one!**

To play the ultimate golf quiz, split players into two teams. Each team should nominate one player to read the questions. Team 1 should choose a page in the book and read the questions on that page to Team 2. Team 2 should then choose another page and read the questions on that page to Team 1.

At the end of the game count how many points each team has scored – the team with the highest score is the winner!

On which courses would you find the following features?

A) Rae's Creek

B) Burma Road

C) Well Well

D) Tickly Tap

E) Bobby Jones

F) Babe in the Woods

G) The Postage Stamp

H) The Cardinal Bunker

1

How many...?

A) Pimples on a golf ball

B) Strokes would you have to take to get par on a 197-yard hole

C) Greens at St Andrews

D) Golfers are invited each year to compete in the World Matchplay Championship

E) Golfers represent their continent in each Ryder Cup

F) Strokes did Herman Tissies take at the Postage Stamp, Royal Troon, during the 1950 British Open

G) Majors did Ben Hogan win

H) Holes were there on the original St Andrews course

2

What nationality is...?

A) Vijay Singh

B) David Duval

C) Lee Westwood

D) Colin Montgomerie

E) Costantino Rocca

F) José Maria Cañizares

G) Ian Woosnam

H) Sven Strüver

Strange but true.

A) Who won the 1981 US Amateur Championship?

B) In which film did James Bond play golf?

C) Which golfer had back problems after being struck by lightning?

D) How did Joyce Wethered get two birdies at the same hole in 1927?

E) Which US President has been a regular golfing partner of Bob Hope?

F) How did Samuel Ryder of "Ryder Cup" fame make his fortune?

G) Which golfer almost pulled out of the 1993 Ryder Cup after injuring himself sleepwalking?

H) Where does a dog called Fergus chase the Canada geese off the course?

4

Who said...?

A) "Maybe a few pints of Murphy's might do it some good"

B) "Ray Charles could have putted better"

C) "You've just one problem. You stand too close to the ball – after you've hit it"

D) "Luckily I still enjoy practising, which some people don't"

E) "My family were so poor they couldn't have kids. The lady next door had me"

F) "I'd give up golf if I didn't have so many sweaters"

G) "Golf is a good walk spoiled"

H) "To be a champion you have to find a way to get the ball in the cup on the last day"

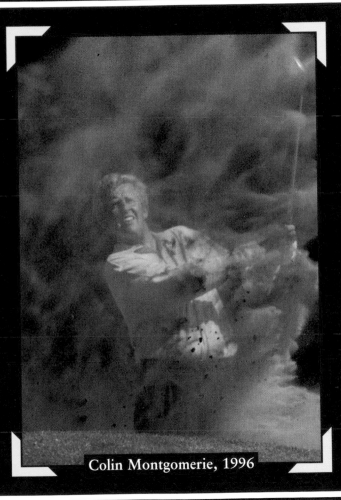

Colin Montgomerie, 1996

Where are the following courses?

A) Valderrama
B) Izumi
C) Pine Valley
D) Druids Glen
E) Wentworth
F) Penina
G) Royal Troon
H) Winged Foot

What do the following terms mean?

A) Bogey

B) Eagle

C) Shagbag

D) Knee-knocker

E) Birdie

F) Albatross

G) Dogleg

H) Carry

Who was the first...?

A) Australian to win the US Open

B) Left-hander to win a
major championship

C) Irishman to win the
British Open

D) Winner of the World
Matchplay Championship

E) Winner of the Ryder Cup

F) Non-American winner of the
US Open

G) Non-British winner of the
British Open

H) Player to amass $1,000,000
in career earnings

8

Name the year when...?

A) Isao Aoki won a home at Gleneagles for a hole-in-one in the World Matchplay Championship

B) Nick Faldo scored a hole-in-one in the Ryder Cup

C) Curtis Strange made his successful defence of the US Open

D) Jack Nicklaus became known as the "Player of the Century"

E) José Maria Olazabal won the US Masters

F) Bernhard Langer won his second Masters title

G) Sandy Lyle won the British Open at Royal St George's, Sandwich

H) GB and Ireland drew with the USA in the Ryder Cup at Royal Birkdale

What is par for each of the following courses?

A) Royal Troon
B) Shinnecock Hills
C) Valderrama
D) Turnberry
E) Royal Melbourne
F) Penina
G) St Andrews
H) Royal Birkdale

Spot the mystery golfer who...

A) Was born in 1914

B) Had a Norwegian father

C) Set her first world athletics javelin record aged 16

D) Won two Olympic gold medals

E) Was the most extraordinary all-round sportswoman that ever lived

F) Won major golf championships on both sides of the Atlantic

G) Was banned from athletics for life after endorsing a sales campaign for a car

H) Died from cancer aged 42

On which course would you find all of the following holes?

- **A)** Westward Ho!
- **B)** Redan
- **C)** Tuckahoe
- **D)** Sebonac
- **E)** Thorn's Elbow
- **F)** Road Side
- **G)** Pump House
- **H)** Pond

Seve Ballesteros, 1991

Name each
golf course

A) It is situated in the Arizona desert

B) It is the European Tour headquarters

C) It was designed by Willie Park
in 1900

D) Each hole is named after a flower,
tree or shrub that grows next to it

E) Sam Torrance sealed the first Ryder
Cup defeat of the Americans for 28
years here

F) It is the oldest in France

G) It was designed by Henry Cotton in
1964 and it later became his home

H) Ailsa Craig and the Isle of Arran can
be seen from here

13

Explain the following terms

A) A forecaddie

B) A whiff

C) The yips

D) A sclaff shot

E) Standard scratch score

F) Topping

G) Fescue

H) A guttie

At what age did...?

A) Tom Morris Junior become the youngest ever winner of the British Open in 1868

B) Gary Player become the then oldest winner of the US Masters in 1978

C) Nick Faldo become the youngest ever competitor in the Ryder Cup

D) Sam Snead win the Greater Greensboro Open in 1965

E) Ray Floyd compete in the Ryder Cup in 1993

F) Seve Ballesteros win the US Masters in 1980

G) Julius Boros win the US PGA Championship in 1968 to become the oldest winner of a Major

H) Coby Orr of Colorado shoot a hole-in-one

Spot the mystery golfer who...?

A) Had his first victory as a professional at the West Lakes Classic in 1976

B) Topped the US money list in 1986, 1990 and 1995

C) Won the European Order of Merit in 1982

D) Was ranked number 1 on the Sony World Ranking at the end of 1986, 1987, 1989, 1990 and 1995

E) Won the 1993 British Open at Royal St George's

F) In 1986 led all four Majors after 54 holes, but won only one of them

G) Has lost play-offs in all four Majors

H) Was born in Queensland, Australia

Which golf clubs have the following names?

A) Spoon

B) Brassie

C) Cleek

D) Mashie-Niblick

E) Blaster

F) Baffie

G) Jigger or Sammy

H) Play-club

Identify the famous past and present players from their nicknames below

A) The Walrus

B) Super Mex

C) Champagne Tony

D) The Maestro

E) The Golden Bear

F) Himself

G) Tiger

H) The Car Park Champion

18

What nationality is...?

A) Retief Goosen
B) Fredrik Jacobsen
C) Nick Faldo
D) Craig Parry
E) Jumbo Ozaki
F) Billy Andrade
G) Marc Farry
H) Gordon Brand Jnr

Nick Faldo, 1995

Who said...?

A) "I know I'm getting better because I'm hitting fewer spectators"

B) "I don't care to join any club that's prepared to have me as a member"

C) "Golf is a better game played downhill"

D) "The person I fear most in the last two rounds is myself"

E) "No one remembers who came second"

F) "I'd like to see the fairways more narrow. Then everybody would have to play from the rough, not just me"

G) "The more I practise, the luckier I get"

H) "Real pressure is playing for $10 when you've only got $5 in your pocket"

Think of a number. What is...?

A) The diameter of a golf hole

B) The maximum number of clubs a player can carry

C) The number of holes over which the British Open is played

D) The minimum depth of the hole

E) An Albatross on a par 5 hole

F) The number of Majors played in a year

G) The yardage for Carnoustie, the longest on the British Open list

H) A woman's maximum handicap

Name each golf course

A) It was Europe's choice of location for the first Ryder Cup to be played outside the UK

B) It is overlooked by the Matterhorn

C) You drive over the Pacific Ocean at its 15th, 16th and 17th holes

D) It is known as "the course that Jack built"

E) It is regarded as the most difficult 18 holes in America

F) It is where the World Golf Hall of Fame is situated

G) It boasts the oldest clubhouse in the US, dating back to 1892

H) It was named after an athletic club emblem

Spot the mystery golfer who...

A) Was the US Ryder Cup team captain in 1985 when the Americans lost

B) Was introduced to golf as a boy, caddying at a local public course

C) Has a middle name of Buck

D) Made six Ryder Cup appearances as a player

E) Won the US Open at his third attempt

F) Is famous for his humorous remarks

G) Was born in 1939 in Dallas, Texas

H) Now plays on the US Senior Tour

Where...?

A) Did George Crump build his famous golf course

B) Did Ben Hogan win his US Open Championship after he was nearly killed in a car crash

C) Did Lee Trevino chip in on the 71st hole to help him win his second British Open title

D) Is the "home" of golf

E) Is the highest golf course in the world

F) Were the first 12 British Opens played

G) Did Alan Shepard hit a golf ball on 6 February 1971

H) Did Tom Kite win his only Major

24

Can you solve the following anagrams? Each one is a golfer

A) Wires to God (American)
B) Won at most (American)
C) One tram cars (Scottish)
D) So I now a man (Welsh)
E) Ham melt on (American)
F) Alf in dock (English)
G) Kippers even jar (Swedish)
H) Room on melting ice (Scottish)

In which year did the following take place?

A) The first US Open

B) Nick Faldo won back-to-back play-offs at Augusta to win the US Masters

C) The first major tournament to be decided by a sudden death play-off

D) Larry Mize chipped in for a birdie to win the US Masters

E) Nils Lied, an Australian meteorologist, recorded a 2,640 yard drive across ice in Antartica

F) Sony World Rankings were introduced

G) Arnold Palmer played a shot from behind a bush to reach the 15th hole at Birkdale and went on to win the British Open title

H) Golf was dropped from the Olympic Games

Greg Norman, 1996

What do the following courses have in common?

A) Deal

B) Hoylake

C) Muirfield

D) Sandwich

E) Portrush

F) Turnberry

G) St Andrews

H) Musselburgh

Explain the following terms

- A) Best ball
- B) Divot
- C) Gimmie
- D) Hook
- E) Approach
- F) Slice
- G) Takeaway
- H) Off scratch

On which golf course would you find all of the following?

A) The Grave
B) The Coffin
C) Principal's Nose
D) Ginger Beer
E) The Valley of Sin
F) Hell Bunker
G) Tom Morris
H) The Road Hole

Who is...?

A) Golfer Graham Marsh's sporting brother

B) The only one-eyed golfer to win the US Open

C) Jeff "Squeaky" Medlan

D) Catherine Lacoste's father

E) George Lyon

F) Alister Mackenzie

G) The golfer featured in the film *Follow the Sun*

H) The only woman to shoot 280 in the US Women's Open

Who said...?

A) "We tournament golfers are much overrated. We get paid too much"

B) "My swing is faultless"

C) "They say I get in too many bunkers. But it is no problem. I am the best bunker player"

D) "I think I fail a bit less than everyone else"

E) "I try to work with God as my partner"

F) "Just knock hell out of it with your right hand"

G) "You can talk to a fade but a hook won't listen"

H) "The reason The Road Hole at St Andrews is the most difficult par 4 in the world is that it was designed as a par 6"

Where are the following courses?

A) Knokke-le-Zoute
B) Glen Abbey
C) Royal Portrush
D) Ballybunion
E) The National
F) The Belfry
G) Crans-sur-Sierre
H) Royal Cape

Explain the following golfing terms

- A) Casual water
- B) Apron
- C) Ace
- D) Fairway
- E) Fore!
- F) Lie
- G) Stance
- H) Lost ball

Constantino Rocca, 1993

Firsts

A) Name the first trophy Gary Player won on British soil

B) Name the first non-Scottish player to win the British Open

C) Name the American amateur who became the first player to win the four major championships in one year

D) In which year was golf first played at St Andrews?

E) Name the author of the first golf text book to include photographs

F) Name the first golfer this century to win three British Opens in a row

G) In which year did Jack Nicklaus first compete professionally in Britain?

H) In which year did Henry Cotton win the first of his three British Opens?

Spot the mystery golfer who...

A) Burst onto the European scene in the Summer of 1976

B) Has won the World Matchplay five times

C) Was the leading European golfer in the late 1970s and early 1980s

D) Won the British Open in 1979, 1984 and 1988

E) Is the most charismatic golfer the European tour has ever produced

F) Became the youngest ever Masters champion in 1980

G) Was the 1997 Ryder Cup captain

H) Was born in Santander in 1957

Strange but true. Who...?

A) Was killed by his own club, after it was thrown in temper

B) Between 1963 and 1964 devised and played the longest hole in the world, 1,978,720 yards coast to coast across America

C) Was the actress and sportswoman who scored a hole-in-one with her first ever tee shot on her first ever round of golf

D) Famously killed a pike with a hooked tee shot at Barnham Broom golf club

E) Devoted his life to playing golf on as many courses as possible – 3,615 in total!

F) Is the ex-President of the United States, notorious for hitting spectators at pro-am and pro-celebrity events

G) Was the British woman who won Wimbledon, the British Ladies' Golf Championship and an Olympic medal at archery

H) Was the professional player that hit 1,817 shots over 16 hours 25 minutes in an attempt to score a hole-in-one, and failed

Who competes for the...?

A) US PGA Championship
B) Solheim Cup
C) Curtis Cup
D) Ryder Cup
E) World Cup of Golf
F) Alfred Dunhill Cup
G) Walker Cup
H) World Matchplay Championship

Name the only golfer to do the following

A) Win the US Women's Open by 12 shots

B) Hit five consecutive shots in the water at the US Masters

C) Win the British Open on five different courses

D) Win three national championships in three weeks

E) Lose the US Open because he hit four shots out of a tree

F) Shoot a 63 during a round of the US Masters

G) Shoot 13 on the 13th hole during the US Masters

H) Fall off a cliff during a pro-am in 1957

Name the golfing authors of the following books

     A) *Play Better Golf*

     B) *Golf Masterclass*

     C) *Play Great Golf*

     D) *The 19th Hole*

     E) *The Golf Swing*

     F) *Your Game and Mine*

     G) *A Swing for Life*

     H) *Golf My Way*

How good is your history?

A) The prototype for the modern golf ball was invented by a Chicago dentist in 1902. Can you name him?

B) In which year was the first British Open played in England?

C) Which English king appointed William Mayne of Edinburgh as royal club-maker?

D) In which year were the rules of golf first written down?

E) Name the oldest established golf club in England

F) From which French word does the term "caddie" originate?

G) What was Gene Sarazen's real name?

H) From which game is golf believed to have originated?

Sam Torrance, 1995

On which course would you find all of the following holes?

A) Gulley
B) Plantation
C) Railway
D) South America
E) Whins
F) Luckyslap
G) Spectacles
H) Southward Ho!

What do the following courses have in common?

A) St Andrews
B) Royal St George's
C) Turnberry
D) Royal Birkdale
E) Muirfield
F) Pebble Beach
G) San Lorenzo
H) Ballybunion

Where was the British Open held in these years?

A) 1998
B) 1994
C) 1995
D) 1989
E) 1975
F) 1980
G) 1988
H) 1993

How much do you know about women's golf?

A) Who did Nancy Lopez marry in 1982?

B) Name the brother of the legendary Joyce Wethered who was also a famous golfer.

C) Who beat Bridget Newell to win the British Women's Amateur Championship at the age of 19 in 1936?

D) How old was Laura Davies when she made her first Curtis Cup appearance in 1984?

E) What offer did Jan Stephenson turn down after winning the LPGA in 1982?

F) When Diane Bailey was presented with the Curtis Cup in 1986, it was the first time Britain and Ireland had won for how many years?

G) Who won both the English Women's Amateur and English Girls' title in 1991?

H) How many US Women's Open titles did Babe Zaharias win?

What nationality is...?

A) Tom Lehman
B) Jarmo Sandelin
C) Joe Ozaki
D) Stephen Ames
E) Steve Elkington
F) Fred Funk
G) Mark James
H) Mark Mouland

Who have the following nicknames?

A) Old Ski-nose

B) The Peacock

C) Poker Face

D) The Gee Wiz Kid

E) Great White Shark

F) The Black Knight

G) Cupcakes

H) Tower

How much do you know about Tiger Woods?

A) Where and in what year was he born?

B) What year did he turn professional?

C) Where did he win his first Major?

D) Who is his coach?

E) Which American university did he attend?

F) What year did he first play in the Ryder Cup?

G) Who beat him in the 1995 Walker Cup singles at Porthcawl?

H) How many times did he win the US Junior Amateur Championship?

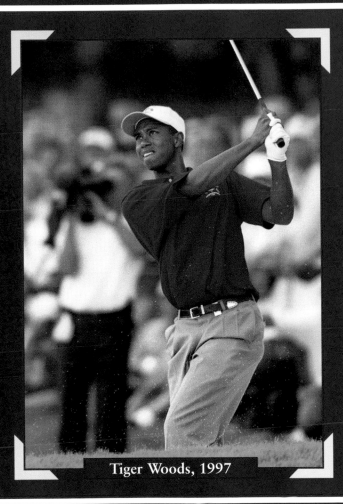

Tiger Woods, 1997

Which annual event is associated with the following venues?

A) Glen Abbey

B) The Belfry

C) Wentworth

D) St Andrews

E) Augusta

F) Sun City

G) Tryall

H) Valderrama

Who said...?

A) "I don't trust doctors. They are like golfers. Everyone has a different answer to your problem."

B) "The most difficult shot in golf? The hole-in-one"

C) "I wear black. I loved westerns and the cowboys always looked good in black"

D) "There's no word for it. Germans don't have 'yips'"

E) "What you must do with anybody who is going to teach you this game is stick with him and have complete faith in him"

F) "Baseball players quit playing and take up golf; basketball players quit and take up golf. What are we supposed to take up when we quit?"

G) "Any golfer worth his salt has to cross the sea and try to win the British Open"

H) "Look like a woman, play like a man"

These golf courses are all in which country?

A) San Lorenzo
B) Troia
C) Penha Longa
D) Pinta
E) Vila Sol
F) Quinta do Lago
G) Praia D'el Rey
H) Aroeira

Solve the anagrams to identify the golfers

A) Event oiler (American)
B) Is foe to green (Swedish)
C) A tunas in goal (Spanish)
D) Tod is fav Dr (South African)
E) Let boss see laver (Spanish)
F) Repeat kerb (English)
G) Rick wasn't ET (American)
H) Loaf on brink (New Zealander)

Where...?

A) Did the first Ryder Cup take place

B) Was the first US Open held

C) Would you find the ruling body of the sport

D) Is Royal Birkdale

E) Is the most northerly golf club in the world

F) Was Nick Price born

G) Was the longest sudden-death play-off in US Tour history (it lasted 11 holes)

H) Was Brett Ogle when he injured himself when his own ball rebounded off a tree and hit his knee

What...?

A) Did husband and wife golfers Harold and Ginny Leyes achieve in 1966

B) Does the US Masters champion receive

C) Is the title of the novel written by Peter Alliss

D) Is a bandit

E) Is the Grand Slam of golf

F) Is the highest score ever recorded at a single hole

G) Did George Grant invent in 1899 which has been used by golfers ever since

H) Colour ball did John Ball use, in order to win a bet, while playing golf in fog in 1907

In 1991, who...?

A) Headed the Sony World Rankings

B) Was John Daly's caddy when he won the US PGA Championship

C) Won the inaugural Johnnie Walker World Championship

D) Won the South African Open

E) Won the World Matchplay Championship

F) Won the Ryder Cup

G) Won the US Open

H) Won the Walker Cup

Jack Nicklaus, 1996

Identify the following golfers. Their surnames begin with W

A) The second youngest player to represent Great Britain in the Ryder Cup

B) The 1977 US PGA Champion

C) The first British golfer to earn £1 million in a year

D) A graduate of psychology

E) The victor at Royal Troon in 1973

F) He donated the cup that is played for by amateur golfers from Great Britain, Ireland and the USA

G) He lost a play-off against Gene Sarazan for the 1935 US Masters

H) He won the first televised US Open in 1947

Who would rather forget these records?

A) A triple triple triple triple bogey during the US Open in 1938

B) A triple whiff at the same hole in 1986

C) Carding an 18 at a par 5 in the Bay Hill Invitational in 1998

D) Finishing runner up the most times at a Major, and never having won

E) Missing the cut twice when defending champion at the US Masters

F) Suffering one of the biggest singles defeats in the Ryder Cup, when losing to Tom Kite in 1989

G) Missing a 2-foot putt that would have made him the 1989 US Masters champion

H) Appearing seven times in the Ryder Cup for Great Britain but never finishing on the winning team

Name the golfer who...

A) Shot himself in the foot during a round

B) Scored a double eagle in the US Open

C) Lost the US Open because he knocked himself out with his own club

D) Lost the US Masters because he signed an incorrect scorecard

E) Hit a drive into his own bag during a professional tournament

F) Scored a birdie for his opponent (his ball hit his partner's ball and both rolled into the hole)

G) Hit a shot into a spectator's bra in a professional tournament

H) Played in the 1998 Solheim Cup when pregnant

In 1994, who won the...?

A) US Amateur Championship

B) Curtis Cup

C) Ladies British Open

D) Players' Championship

E) European Order of Merit

F) Alfred Dunhill Cup

G) US Masters

H) British Open

What nationality is...?

A) Tony Johnstone

B) Padraig Harrington

C) Gary Orr

D) Jong Duck Kim

E) Angel Cabrera

F) Jean Van de Velde

G) Jun Cheng

H) Alex Cejka

Spot the mystery golfer who...?

A) Is a renowned long hitter

B) Was the first Briton to win the US Open

C) Is an MBE

D) Has a passion for fast cars and gambling

E) Was the European Order of Merit winner in 1985 and 1986

F) Was the leading money winner on the LPGA Tour in 1994

G) Won the British Open in 1986

H) Is Britain's most famous female golfer

On which course would you find all of the following holes?

A) Wee Bogle
B) Tappit Hen
C) King's Hame
D) Silver Tassie
E) Broomy Law
F) Deil's Creel
G) Kittle Kink
H) East Neuk

Bernhard Langer, 1995

What do the following terms mean?

A) All square
B) Shaft
C) Nap
D) Break
E) Hosel
F) Hazard
G) Fog
H) Heel

Who...?

A) Is India's only female professional golfer

B) Was the first lady golfer to be mentioned by name

C) Holds the record highest score (of 23) for one hole at a professional tournament

D) Was the first black golfer to win the US Amateur Championship

E) Is the winner of the British Open who was tried for attempted murder in 1970

F) Won the 1998 US Masters and British Open

G) Was the leading amateur in the 1998 British Open

H) Was described by the *Chicago Tribune* as 'even longer than War and Peace'

Can you identify the mystery golfer?

A) His nickname is Huckleberry Dillinger

B) He won his first British Open in 1975

C) His manager is his brother-in-law

D) He once said: "Charisma is winning major championships."

E) He made his Ryder Cup debut in 1977

F) He graduated from Stanford University with a degree in psychology

G) He won the Masters for a second time in 1981

H) He was born in Kansas City on the 4th of September 1959

64

In 1975, who...?

A) Won the US PGA Championship

B) Won the US Masters

C) Won the British Open

D) Beat Jack Nicklaus twice in Ryder Cup singles

E) Headed the European Order of Merit

F) Won the World Matchplay Championship

G) Won the Australian Open

H) Won the South African Open

Strange but true...

A) Harry Bradshaw played a memorable shot in the 1949 British Open. Where was the ball lying?

B) How do you qualify for the Bobby Jones Classic?

C) What was Tiger Wood's best score for 9 holes as a 3-year-old?

D) Two golfers were struck by lightning in 1977, one in the Swiss Open and one in the Scandinavian Open. Who were they?

E) Playing at the John O'Gaunt Golf Club, Bedfordshire, a member hit a drive that did not touch the ground for 40 miles. How?

F) Where is the highest golf course in the world?

G) How many holes-in-one were there in the 1981 British Open?

H) How many putts did Dave Hill take on the 5th green in the 1962 US Open?

The World Matchplay Championships

A) What year was it first held?

B) In the first year of the Championship's existence, how much was the winner's prize money?

C) Who was the first Japanese player to be invited to take part?

D) Which is the shortest hole at Wentworth?

E) Which is the longest hole at Wentworth?

F) Who won three times in succession in the 1990s?

G) Name the two players that have won five times

H) Who was the first British golfer to win the title?

Where...?

A) Is the highest course in Europe

B) Is the longest hole in the world

C) Was the 1998 Solheim Cup played

D) Is the longest hole in British Open Championship golf

E) Will the British Open be held in the year 2000

F) Did Jack Nicklaus design and build a new course named The Heritage

G) Is home for the LPGA sensation Does Se Ri Pak

H) Is home for the leading amateur Matthew Kuchar?

Mark O'Meara, 1997

What are the rulings in the following situations?

A) An animal picks up your ball and runs away with it

B) Your ball comes to rest next to a sprinkler head

C) You play the wrong ball in a hazard

D) You play the wrong ball on the fairway

E) The ball topples off the tee while you are in your backswing

F) Your drive comes to rest close to a drinks can

G) On the tee your partner treads down the grass behind the ball

H) You drive out of bounds off the tee

Vital statistics

A) Name the top three in the 1997 World Golf rankings in descending order

B) Nick Faldo's PGA Tour earnings in 1997 topped $500,000 – true or false?

C) Who won the 1997 Buick Championship?

D) Who finished third in the 1997 US Open?

E) Whose first win was the 1987 MCI Heritage Classic?

F) Name both captains of the 1995 Ryder Cup teams?

G) Who beat Ben Crenshaw in a play-off to win the 1992 Byron Nelson Classic?

H) Name the top three in the 1997 World PGA Tour money list.

70

Solutions

P1 **A)** Augusta **B)** Wentworth **C)** Winged Foot
D) Turnberry **E)** St Andrews **F)** Winged Foot
G) Troon **H)** Prestwick

P2 **A)** 336 **B)** 3 **C)** 11 **D)** 12 **E)** 12 **F)** 15 **G)** 9
H) 22

P3 **A)** Fijian **B)** American **C)** English **D)** Scottish
E) Italian **F)** Spanish **G)** Welsh **H)** German

P4 **A)** Nathaniel Crosby, son of Bing **B)** *Goldfinger*
C) Lee Trevino **D)** Her drive hit a swallow, the
hole was birdied **E)** Gerald Ford **F)** Selling flower
seed **G)** Sam Torrance **H)** Sahalee GC

P5 **A)** Ernie Els (treatment for his back injury!)
B) Lee Trevino **C)** Sam Snead **D)** Bernhard
Langer **E)** Lee Trevino **F)** Bob Hope
G) Mark Twain **H)** Tom Watson

P6 **A)** Spain **B)** Japan **C)** New Jersey, USA
D) Dublin, Eire **E)** Surrey, England **F)** Algarve,
Portugal **G)** Ayr, Scotland **H)** Near New York,
USA

P7 **A)** 1 over par **B)** 2 under par **C)** A practice ball
bag **D)** A very short putt **E)** 1 under par **F)** 3
under par **G)** A fairway that has a change of
direction **H)** The distance the ball travels in
the air

P8 **A)** David Graham **B)** Bob Charles **C)** Fred Daly

Solutions

D) Arnold Palmer E) USA F) Harry Vardon
(GB, 1900) G) Arnaud Massy (France, 1901)
H) Arnold Palmer

P9 A) 1979 B) 1993 C) 1989 D) 1988 E) 1994
F) 1993 G) 1985 H) 1969

P10 A) 72 B) 70 C) 71 D) 70 E) 71 F) 73
G) 72 H) 70

P11 Babe Zaharias (born Mildred Didrikson)

P12 Shinnecock Hills

P13 A) Desert Highlands B) Wentworth
C) Sunningdale D) Augusta E) The Belfry
F) Chantilly G) Penina H) Turnberry

P14 A) A ball spotter at blind holes B) An air shot
C) Putting problems D) Hitting the ground before
the ball E) A system of handicap rating F) Hitting
the ball above centre G) A type of grass used on
greens H) A type of ball

P15 A) 17 B) 42 C) 20 D) 52 E) 51 F) 23
G) 48 H) 5

P16 Greg Norman

P17 A) 3-wood B) 2-wood C) 1-iron D) 7-iron
E) Sand wedge F) 4-wood G) 4-iron H) Driver

P18 A) Craig Stadler B) Lee Trevino C) Tony Lema

Solutions

D) Henry Cotton **E)** Jack Nicklaus
F) Christy O'Connor (Snr) **G)** Eldrick Woods
H) Seve Ballesteros

P19 **A)** South African **B)** Swedish **C)** English
D) Australian **E)** Japanese **F)** American
G) French **H)** Scottish

P20 **A)** Gerald Ford **B)** Groucho Marx **C)** Jack
Nicklaus **D)** Tom Watson **E)** Walter Hagan
F) Seve Ballesteros **G)** Gary Player **H)** Lee
Trevino

P21 **A)** 4 $^1/_4$ inches **B)** 14 **C)** 72 **D)** 4 inches **E)** 2
F) 4 **G)** 7,066 yards **H)** 36

P22 **A)** Valderrama **B)** Crans-sur-Sierre **C)** Cypress
Point **D)** Muirfield Village **E)** Oakmont
F) Pinehurst **G)** Shinnecock Hills **H)** Winged
Foot

P23 Lee Trevino

P24 **A)** Pine Valley **B)** Merion **C)** Muirfield
D) St Andrews **E)** Tucty Golf Club in Morococha,
Peru – 14,335 feet above sea level at its lowest
point **F)** Prestwick, Scotland **G)** On the moon
H) Pebble Beach

P25 **A)** Tiger Woods **B)** Tom Watson **C)** Sam Torrance
D) Ian Woosnam **E)** Tom Lehman **F)** Nick Faldo
G) Jesper Parnevik **H)** Colin Montgomerie

Solutions

P26 **A)** 1895 **B)** 1989/90 **C)** 1977 (at Pebble Beach)
D) 1987 **E)** 1962 **F)** 1986 **G)** 1961 **H)** 1908

P27 They have all hosted the British Open

P28 **A)** A match where 1 player competes against 2 or
3 others **B)** A piece of turf cut away when playing
a stroke; it must be replaced **C)** A putt short
enough to be conceded **D)** For a right-handed
player, a shot where the ball travels well left of the
target **E)** A shot from fairway to green **F)** For a
right-handed player, a shot where the ball travels
well to the right of the target **G)** The first
movement of the club in the backswing
H) Playing with a handicap of O

P29 St Andrews

P30 **A)** Rodney Marsh (Australian cricketer)
B) Tommy Armour **C)** Nick Price's regular caddy
in the early 1990s **D)** The tennis player Rene
Lacoste **E)** The winner of the last golf gold medal
presented at the Olympics **F)** The designer of
Augusta and Royal Melbourne golf courses
G) Ben Hogan **H)** Amy Alcott

P31 **A)** Tom Watson **B)** Ian Woosnam **C)** Seve
Ballesteros **D)** Jack Nicklaus **E)** Gary Player
F) Tommy Armour **G)** Lee Trevino
H) Ben Crenshaw

Solutions

P32 **A)** Belgium **B)** Oakville, Canada **C)** Northern Ireland **D)** County Kerry, Eire **E)** Ontario, Canada **F)** Sutton Coldfield, England **G)** Switzerland **H)** Cape Town, South Africa

P33 **A)** Temporary water on the course **B)** The area around the green **C)** A hole-in-one **D)** The area between tee and green **E)** A warning shout **F)** The position in which the ball comes to rest **G)** The position a player adopts prior to hitting the ball **H)** A ball is deemed lost if it is not found within 5 minutes of starting to look for it

P34 **A)** The Dunlop in 1956 **B)** Englishman Jack Burns in 1888 **C)** Bobby Jones **D)** 1754 **E)** "Long Jim" Barnes **F)** Peter Thomson **G)** 1962 **H)** 1934

P35 Seve Ballesteros

P36 **A)** Michael Scaglione **B)** Floyd Scatterlee Rood **C)** Gertrude Lawrence **D)** Les King **E)** Ralph Kennedy **F)** Gerald Ford **G)** Charlotte Dod **H)** Harry Gonder

P37 **A)** Players qualified from the US Tour **B)** Women professionals from the US and Europe **C)** Women amateurs from the US, Great Britain and Ireland **D)** American and European male professionals **E)** No more than 50 male players who have won designated qualifying tournaments around the

Solutions

world **F)** Teams of three from countries around the world **G)** Male amateurs from the US, Great Britain and Ireland **H)** 12 invited players

P38 **A)** Babe Zaharias **B)** Tom Weiskopf **C)** Tom Watson **D)** Lee Trevino **E)** Phil Rodgers **F)** Nick Price
G) Tommy Nakajima **H)** Tony Lema

P39 **A)** Peter Alliss **B)** Christy O'Connor **C)** Arnold Palmer **D)** Bernard Gallacher **E)** David Leadbetter **F)** Tony Jacklin **G)** Nick Faldo **H)** Jack Nicklaus

P40 **A)** Dr Haskell **B)** 1894 (Sandwich) **C)** James I **D)** 1744 **E)** Blackheath **F)** Cadet **G)** Eugene Saraceni **H)** Qui wan

P41 Carnoustie

P42 They are all links courses

P43 **A)** Royal Birkdale **B)** Turnberry **C)** St Andrews **D)** Royal Troon **E)** Carnoustie **F)** Muirfield **G)** Royal Lytham & St Anne's **H)** Royal St George's, Sandwich

P44 **A)** Ray Knight, a baseball star **B)** Roger **C)** Pam Barton **D)** 20 **E)** $150,000 to pose nude for Playboy **F)** 30 **G)** Nikki Buxton **H)** 3

P45 **A)** American **B)** Swedish **C)** Japanese

Solutions

D) Trinidadian E) Australian F) American
G) English H) Welsh

P46 A) Bob Hope B) Payne Stewart C) Paul Way
D) Paul Azinger E) Greg Norman F) Gary Player
G) Fred Couples H) Isao Aoki

P47 A) Cypress, California (Dec 1975) B) 1996
C) Augusta (1997) D) Butch Harmon E) Stanford
F) 1997 G) Gary Wolstenholme H) 3 (1991/2/3)

P48 A) Canadian Open B) The English Open
C) The World Matchplay Championships
D) The Alfred Dunhill Cup E) The US Masters
F) The Million Dollar Challenge G) The Johnnie
Walker World Championship H) The Volvo
Masters

P49 A) Seve Ballesteros B) Groucho Marx
C) Gary Player D) Bernhard Langer E) Nick Faldo
(of David Leadbetter) F) Lee Trevino
G) Jack Nicklaus H) Jan Stephenson

P50 Portugal

P51 A) Lee Trevino B) Retief Goosen C) Santiago
Luna D) David Frost E) Seve Ballesteros
F) Peter Baker G) Stewart Cink H) Frank Nobilo

P52 A) Worcester, Massachusetts B) Newport, Rhode
Island C) St Andrews (the Royal & Ancient)
D) Southport, Lancashire E) Akereyri, Iceland

Solutions

F) Durban, South Africa G) At the Motor City Open (in 1949) H) Sydney, Australia

P53 A) They both scored holes-in-one at the same hole on the same day B) The green jacket
C) *The Duke* D) A golfer who plays below his current handicap E) Winning all 4 Majors in the same year F) 166 (many of the strokes were played from a rowing boat as the ball floated 1 $\frac{1}{2}$ miles down a river!) G) The tee H) Black

P54 A) Ian Woosnam B) Jeff "Squeaky" Medlen
C) Fred Couples D) Wayne Westner E) Seve Ballesteros F) USA G) Payne Stewart H) USA

P55 A) Paul Way B) Lanny Wadkins C) Ian Woosnam
D) Tom Watson E) Tom Weiskopf F) George Walker G) Craig Wood H) Lew Worsham

P56 A) Ray Ainsley B) Al Chandler C) John Daly
D) Harry Cooper E) Seve Ballesteros F) Howard Clark G) Scott Hoch H) Tony Jacklin

P57 A) Al Capone B) Tze-Chung Chen C) Bobby Cruickshank D) Roberto De Vicenzo
E) Raymond Floyd F) Jimmy Hines
G) Hale Irwin H) Tammy Green

P58 A) Tiger Woods B) It was shared between Great Britain, Ireland and America C) Liselotte Neumann (Sweden) D) Greg Norman E) Colin

Solutions

Montgomerie **F)** Canada **G)** José Maria Olazabal **H)** Nick Price

P59 **A)** Zimbabwean **B)** Irish **C)** Scottish **D)** Korean **E)** Argentinian **F)** French **G)** Chinese **H)** German

P60 Laura Davies

P61 Gleneagles

P62 **A)** When a game is tied **B)** The stick or handle of a club **C)** The way the grass lies on a green **D)** The distance a putt might turn **E)** The socket in a club into which the shaft fits **F)** A general term for bunker, long grass, road, water etc **G)** Moss or rank grass **H)** The part of the club nearest the hosel

P63 **A)** Smrita Mehra **B)** Mary Queen of Scots **C)** Tommy Armour **D)** Tiger Woods **E)** Bobby Locke **F)** Mark O'Meara **G)** Justin Rose **H)** John Daly

P64 Tom Watson

P65 **A)** Jack Nicklaus **B)** Jack Nicklaus **C)** Tom Watson **D)** Brian Barnes **E)** Dale Hayes **F)** Hale Irwin **G)** Jack Nicklaus **H)** Gary Player

P66 **A)** In a broken bottle **B)** You must be called Bobby Jones **C)** 48 **D)** Mark James, Seve Ballesteros **E)** The ball landed in a truck travelling

Solutions

to London **F)** Tectu Golf Club, Peru (14,335 feet)
G) 3 **H)** 6

P67 **A)** 1964 **B)** £5,000 **C)** Isao Aoki **D)** Hole 2, par
3, 155yards **E)** Hole 17, par 5,571 yards
F) Ernie Els **G)** Gary Player and Seve Ballesteros
H) Ian Woosnam

P68 **A)** Sestriere, Italy (6,500 feet) **B)** 7th at Satsuki
Golf Course, Sanno, Japan (881 metres long)
C) Muirfield Village, Ohio **D)** 6th at Royal Troon
(577 yards) **E)** St Andrews **F)** At the New
London GC **G)** Korea **H)** America

P69 **A)** Replace with another ball – no penalty
B) Identify nearest point of relief, drop ball within
one club's length, no nearer the hole – no penalty
C) Identify your own – no penalty **D)** Replace ball
– penalty stroke **E)** Stop, replace ball – no penalty
F) The can is classed as a 'moveable obstruction',
so remove can and play on – no penalty
G) This is allowed on the tee, but nowhere else
H) Penalty – play 3rd shot from the tee

P70 **A)** Greg Norman, Tiger Woods, Nick Price
B) False – he won $431,326 **C)** Ernie Els
D) Tom Lehman **E)** Davis Love III **F)** Lanny
Wadkins and Bernhard Gallacher **G)** Billy Ray
Brown **H)** Tiger Woods, David Duval, Ernie Els